Unless Recalled Earlier

THE ANDERSONVILLE PRISON CIVIL WAR CRIMES TRIAL

A Headline Court Case

Headline Court Cases

The Andersonville Prison Civil War Crimes Trial
A Headline Court Case
0-7660-1386-3

The John Brown Slavery Revolt Trial
A Headline Court Case
0-7660-1385-5

The Lindbergh Baby Kidnapping Trial
A Headline Court Case
0-7660-1389-8

The Lizzie Borden "Axe Murder" Trial
A Headline Court Case
0-7660-1422-3

The Nuremberg Nazi War Crimes Trials
A Headline Court Case
0-7660-1384-7

The Sacco and Vanzetti Controversial Murder Trial
A Headline Court Case
0-7660-1387-1

The Salem Witchcraft Trials
A Headline Court Case
0-7660-1383-9

The Scopes Monkey Trial
A Headline Court Case
0-7660-1388-X

THE ANDERSONVILLE PRISON CIVIL WAR CRIMES TRIAL

A Headline Court Case

Susan Banfield

Enslow Publishers, Inc.

40 Industrial Road	PO Box 38
Box 398	Aldershot
Berkeley Heights, NJ 07922	Hants GU12 6BP
USA	UK

http://www.enslow.com

Library of Congress Cataloging-in-Publication Data

Banfield, Susan
  The Andersonville Prison Civil War crimes trial : a headline court
case / Susan Banfield.
     p. cm. — (Headline court cases)
  Includes bibliographical references and index.
  Summary: Examines the war crimes trial in which Henry Wirz, the
Confederate officer in charge of Andersonville Prison camp, was accused
of allowing the prisoners to be deliberately abused and neglected.
  ISBN 0-7660-1386-3
  1. Wirz, Henry, 1823?–1865—Trials, litigation, etc.—Juvenile
literature. 2. War crimes trials—Georgia—Andersonville—Juvenile
literature. 3. Prisoners of war—Georgia—Andersonville—Juvenile
literature. 4. Andersonville Prison—Juvenile literature. 5. United
States—History—Civil War, 1861–1865—Prisoners and prisons—Juvenile
literature. [1. Wirz, Henry, 1823?–1865—Trials, litigation, etc. 2. War
crime trials—Georgia—Andersonville. 3. Andersonville Prison.
4. United States—History—Civil War, 1861–1865—Prisoners and prisons.]
I. Title. II. Series.
  KF223.W57B36   2000
  345.73'0238—dc21
                                                        00-008297

Printed in the United States of America

10 9 8 7 6 5 4 3 2 1

To Our Readers:
All Internet addresses in this book were active and appropriate when we went to press.
Any comments or suggestions can be sent by e-mail to Comments@enslow.com or to
the address on the back cover.

Photo Credits: Andersonville National Historic Site, 84; The Confederate
Veteran, p. 65; Library of Congress, pp. 3, 10, 15, 22, 26, 31, 38, 42, 49, 53, 57,
68, 75, 79; National Archives, p. 88.

Cover Photo: National Archives

Contents

chapter one

DRAMA IN THE COURTROOM

WASHINGTON, D.C.— Quiet tension filled the courtroom. The gas light of the chandelier flickered off the brass buttons of the men in crisp military uniforms seated in the center. It cast shadows on the somber faces of the men and women who packed the room. Except for the scratching of the reporters' pens, the voice of the witness on the stand was the only sound that could be heard.

That witness, George W. Gray, had identified himself as a soldier in the United States Army, Seventh Indiana Cavalry. He was describing an incident that had occurred while he was imprisoned in the Confederate (Southern) prison at Andersonville, Georgia, during the last year of the Civil War. He told how he had attempted to escape but was captured by a pack of dogs and was then forced— by order of the prison commander, Captain Henry Wirz—to spend time in the stocks:

> I remained for four days, with my feet placed in a block and another lever

placed over my legs, with my arms thrown back, and a chain running across my arms. I remained four days there in the sun; that was my punishment for trying to get away from the prison. At the same time a young man was placed in the stocks—the third man from me. He died there. He was a little sick when he went in, and he died there. . . . The negroes took him out of the stocks after he was dead, threw him into the wagon, and hauled him away.[1]

As if this image of a sick man left to bake to death in the scorching sun of southern Georgia were not sufficiently horrible, the general who was acting as prosecutor (attorney for the government) then asked the witness, "Do you know anything about the commander [Wirz] having shot a prisoner of war there at any time?" There was a hush as Gray began to speak:

He shot a young fellow named William Stewart, a private belonging to the 9th Minnesota Infantry. He and I went out of the stockade with a dead body, and after laying the dead body in the dead-house, Captain Wirz rode up to us and asked by what authority we were out there or what we were doing there. Stewart said we were there by proper authority. Wirz said no more, but drew a revolver and shot the man. After he was killed, the guard took from the body about twenty or thirty dollars, and Wirz took the money from the guard and rode off, telling the guard to take me to prison.[2]

The prosecutor continued to question the witness about exactly what he was doing outside of the prison and about other details of the incident. He then motioned to a sickly looking, dark-haired man who was lying on a couch to the side of the table where the military men were seated. He asked the man to stand. The man raised himself up partway, propped on his elbow. "Do you recognize that man as the person who shot your comrade?" the general asked the witness. "That is the man," Gray answered. No sooner had the witness gotten the words out of his mouth than the man on the couch began blurting out something in response. But he was immediately quieted by order of the general and commanded to stand erect. This he did, but it was a huge effort, and the poor man, clearly distraught, appeared ready to faint. "I think that is the man," Gray repeated.[3]

The testimony of George Gray was one of a number of dramatic moments in the court-martial of Captain Henry Wirz. Wirz had been the Confederate officer in charge of Andersonville Prison during the last year of the Civil War. Under his leadership, more than twelve thousand of the thirty-three thousand Union (Northern) soldiers imprisoned there died—mostly as a result of exposure to sun and rain, insufficient food, and horribly unsanitary conditions—but also as a result of cruel treatment.[4] After the war ended, Wirz was tried by a specially appointed military court for having been at least partially, and in many cases fully and directly, responsible for these deaths.

The trial was immensely controversial, both at the time and for decades afterward. The North had been shocked to learn of the treatment its soldiers had been subjected to in Andersonville Prison, a place that to this day remains a symbol of the horrors of wartime cruelty. There was a strong sense that someone should be made to pay. Many who witnessed Wirz's trial, however, felt that it was full of

Captain Henry Wirz was the Confederate officer in charge of Andersonville Prison during the last year of the Civil War.

irregularities and injustices. They felt that Wirz had been unfairly made a scapegoat for Northern anger.

George Gray's testimony, for example, was some of the most damaging of the whole trial. The Indiana private testified that he had witnessed a man dying in the stocks by direct order of Wirz. He also claimed to have seen Wirz murder a man by his own hand—a man he could call by name. Wirz's emotional reaction to Gray's testimony and his dramatic attempt to respond were interpreted, particularly by Northern newspaper reporters, as an indication of his guilt.[5] Yet others said that in his attempt to speak, Wirz was protesting the fact that what Gray had to say was an out-and-out lie. George Gray, Wirz's sympathizers maintained, was just one of many witnesses who perjured themselves (lied under oath) on the stand in order to secure a conviction.[6]

The story of Andersonville is one that fills those who hear it with horror. Assigning legal blame for one of history's most notorious cases of cruelty and inhumanity is not an easy matter. This case challenged jurors in 1865 and has continued to be a challenge to this day.

chapter two

AMERICAN PRISONERS OF WAR

CIVIL WAR—From 1861 to 1865 the United States was torn apart by a war between its Northern and Southern states. The Southern states, which included Alabama, Arkansas, Florida, Georgia, Louisiana, Mississippi, North Carolina, South Carolina, Tennessee, Texas, and Virginia, withdrew from the Union—the government of the United States—and formed a government of their own called the Confederacy. The Confederate states felt that the federal government was wrongfully forbidding states the right to set their own policies on certain matters. One of the most important of these matters was how African Americans were to be treated. Most people in the Southern states felt that African Americans should remain slaves. Racial prejudice helped Southern whites to consider blacks as inferior property, not human beings.

The Northern states included California, Connecticut, Delaware, Illinois, Indiana, Iowa, Kansas, Kentucky, Maine, Maryland, Massachusetts, Michigan, Minnesota, Missouri, New Hampshire, New Jersey, New York, Ohio, Oregon,

Pennsylvania, Rhode Island, and Vermont. These states were known as the Union. Most Northerners wanted to limit the growth of slavery, and a minority did so because they considered it a moral wrong. Most important, they believed that it was crucial for the country to remain unified and that individual states should not be allowed to divide the United States into a number of different governments.

The War Between the States, also called the Civil War, took a terrible toll on the United States. It cost the Southern states more than a billion dollars and the Northern states several times that amount. It left farms, railroads, and entire cities in ruins. The most tragic cost of all, however, was the cost in human lives. It is estimated that the total casualties came to well over six hundred thousand American lives.[1] Of all the wars that the United States has fought in, only World War II claimed more American lives.

Most of the thousands who were killed in the war died in battle or from wounds received on the battlefield. Many, however—approximately fifty-six thousand—died in the camps constructed in both the North and the South to house the prisoners of war.[2]

At the beginning of the Civil War, prisoners were often exchanged between the two sides at the end of a battle—a private for a private, a sergeant for a sergeant. In July 1862 a formal agreement was worked out between the Union and the Confederacy arranging for the exchange and parole of prisoners of war. (When a prisoner of war is let go on parole, it means that he is given his freedom on the promise that he will no longer take part in the fighting.) But within months, problems had developed with the new arrangement. The North became angry when it learned that the Confederacy would not exchange or parole African-American soldiers who had been taken prisoner. Instead, it planned to make them slaves. The South also threatened to execute any captured officer who had commanded African-American troops. Union officers also discovered that Confederate prisoners whom the North had released on parole were rejoining the Confederate army. Because of these violations of the prisoner exchange agreement, Northern officials stopped the exchanges.

The result of the cease in prisoner exchanges was that both sides in the conflict suddenly had to find a way to deal with the thousands of men being captured in battle. A number of new prison camps were constructed in both the North and the South. Still, many of the prison camps were badly overcrowded and mismanaged, and the prisoners were poorly treated.

Camp Douglas in Chicago, for example, held more than thirty thousand Confederate prisoners. Of those, some thirty-seven hundred died.[3] Most of the deaths were due to the cold, as the men had inadequate clothing and blankets. At Camp Morton in Indianapolis, Confederate prisoners also had inadequate blankets and clothing. In addition, the barracks were run down and food was scarce. Of the twelve thousand men held prisoner at Camp Morton, more than seventeen hundred died.[4] The cold was also responsible for many Confederate deaths at Camp Elmira in New York State. There, prisoners at times had to endure temperatures of ten to fifteen degrees below zero—often without benefit of stoves in their barracks. Of the more than twelve thousand prisoners at Camp Elmira, almost three thousand died.[5] Overall, of the Confederate soldiers taken prisoner in the North, approximately twenty-six thousand died.[6]

The death rate in Southern prisons was even higher than it was in the North. Of the close to two hundred thousand Union soldiers taken prisoner, more than thirty thousand died in Confederate prisoner-of-war camps.[7] Libby Prison in Richmond, Virginia, was the site of more than sixty-two hundred Union deaths.[8] The prisoners there slept on the floor and suffered from the foul air that arose from the four toilets available to the men. At a number of Confederate

A bird's-eye view of Andersonville Prison is shown here. Witnesses such as George Gray described the horrific conditions at Andersonville and the terrible treatment the prisoners received.

prisons, including Camp Florence in South Carolina and Camp Lawton and Andersonville in Georgia, no barracks were provided for the men. They had to construct whatever shelters they could from timber they could find within the stockade.[9]

The treatment of prisoners of war has varied considerably throughout history. In the era directly preceding the Civil War, humane treatment of prisoners was generally recommended. According to one writer,

> When an antagonist no longer resists, there can no longer be any right to use violence towards him; and . . . the belligerent [group at war] cannot refuse to give quarter [shelter] without a direct violation of the law of nature, which warrants [allows] no further hardships towards prisoners than is required by the purposes of safe custody and security.[10]

While legal scholars were arguing that prisoners of war deserved humane treatment, actual American prisoners received something less than that during both the Revolutionary War and the War of 1812. During the Revolutionary War, twenty thousand soldiers of the colonial army were taken prisoner by the British.[11] Some of these men were exchanged, but most were held in British jails or on British prison ships. Eighty-five hundred men died in captivity.[12] During the beginning of the War of 1812, American prisoners of war were once again held captive on British prison ships. However, in 1813 they were transferred to prisons back in England. The death rate in the English prisons was better than it had been on the ships during the Revolutionary War.[13] Still, the prisoners' existence was far from pleasant. As one American wrote of his stay at Dartmoor Prison, "Death itself, with hopes of an hereafter, seemed less terrible than this gloomy prison."[14]

The experiences of prisoners of war during the Civil War were horrific, however. Those in authority were moved to take action to guarantee that, in the future, the actual treatment of such prisoners would be more in line with the humane principles that the legal scholars were urging. Nothing did more to fuel this movement than the story of Andersonville Prison.

chapter three

CONDITIONS AT ANDERSONVILLE

PRISON LIFE—Pine trees stood tall and thick on land crisscrossed by streams. Large fields of corn, vegetables, and grass occasionally broke up the pines, creating a pleasing landscape. The sun was blistering in summer, but the lush green of the trees and the underbrush softened the harsh rays some.

This was southwestern Georgia, the area selected in late 1863 by the Confederate government as the location for a new prison. It would be far from the fighting that was going on in Virginia and large enough to hold some ten thousand prisoners. Captain W. S. Winder was put in charge of determining the actual site. Winder investigated several parts of southwestern Georgia and finally settled on a site near the village of Andersonville. Timber, water, and fertile land for growing crops were all plentiful in the area. The Southwestern Railroad also had a station in Andersonville.[1]

Construction began in January 1864, with slaves providing most of the labor.

They felled local pine trees and cut them to a length of about twenty feet. These were then sunk in the ground next to one another to a depth of five feet, forming a stockade that was fifteen feet high. For security, the slaves built a double wall around the sixteen-acre site and erected eighty sentry boxes (boxes about twelve feet off the ground, in which soldiers with guns stood guard) located at regular intervals around the wall. There was also what was called a "deadline" erected eighteen feet inside the inner stockade.[2] The deadline was a railing that the prisoners would be ordered not to cross under threat of being shot.

The slaves built no barracks or other buildings to house the prisoners. A local planter and lawyer, Ambrose Spencer, happened to notice the absence of shelter while watching the construction and remarked on it to Captain Winder:

> I inquired of W.S. Winder if . . . he was going to erect barracks or shelter of any kind. He replied that he was not; that the damned Yankees who would be put in there would have no need of them. I asked him why he was cutting down all the trees, and suggested that they would prove a shelter to the prisoners, from the heat of the sun at least. He made this reply, or something similar to it: "That is just what I am going to do; I am going to build a pen here that will kill more damned Yankees than can be destroyed in the front." Those are very nearly his words or equivalent to them.[3]

Spencer was also able to describe the kind of weather that the prisoners would experience. As a planter, he was in the habit of keeping track of daily temperatures. In the summer of 1864, the thermometer read as high as 110°F in the shade, he said. The following winter, temperatures would fall as low as 20° or 22°F.[4]

Spencer's conversation with Winder was later used as evidence in the *Wirz* trial. At the very least, it suggests that the Confederate officers in charge of the prison did not always have the welfare of the prisoners in mind.

The first prisoners arrived at Andersonville in late February 1864, before the stockade was even finished and with food and equipment in short supply. That first group of five hundred men was soon followed by groups of hundreds more, until new prisoners were arriving at the rate of approximately four hundred per day.[5]

When the construction of Andersonville was just beginning, Captain Henry Wirz was on his way back from Europe, where for two years he had been a special adviser of Confederate president Jefferson Davis. Wirz had been selected for the mission because he had grown up in Switzerland and was fluent in English, French, and German.[6]

At some point in the late 1840s, Wirz had run into trouble with the law. Although the exact nature of the offense is not known, it involved money. Wirz was sent to prison for a short while, and his wife, whom he had recently married, divorced him. By 1849 Wirz was heartbroken over the loss of his wife, was disgraced by his prison stint, and was at odds with his father, who wanted him to go into business rather than medicine, which Wirz preferred. Wirz then decided to move to the United States.[7] He settled in Kentucky and found work in the medical field. In 1854 he remarried, this time choosing a widow named Elizabeth Wolfe who had two daughters, Susie and Cornelia. After moving the family to Louisiana, in 1855 Wirz and his new wife had a daughter of their own, Cora.[8]

When the Civil War broke out, Wirz enlisted in the Louisiana Volunteers, Company A, Fourth Battalion. His right arm was badly wounded during the Battle of Seven Pines. His arm gave him trouble for the rest of his life. While receiving a promotion to captain "for bravery on [the] battlefield," Wirz had been forced, because of his wound, to retire from active duty on the front. Instead, he was assigned to take charge of Confederate prisoner-of-war camps.[9]

Although this assignment was cut short by his special mission abroad for President Davis, Wirz's experience at supervising prisons led to his selection as the officer assigned to take charge of Andersonville Prison in late March 1864. He moved there with his wife and daughters the following month.[10]

By the time Wirz arrived at Andersonville, the prison was already at its ten-thousand-man capacity, and conditions were greatly deteriorated.[11] Most men, even though they had seen the horrors of the battlefield, were shocked at the sights that greeted them on their arrival at Andersonville. Robert Kellogg, a Connecticut soldier who spent six months in the Georgia prison, described his reactions on first glimpsing the camp:

> As we entered the place a spectacle met our eyes that almost froze our blood with horror, and made our hearts fail within us. Before us were forms that had once been active and

erect;— . . . now nothing but mere walking skeletons, covered with filth and vermin. Many of our men, in the heat and intensity of their feeling, exclaimed with earnestness, "Can this be hell? God protect us!"[12]

The smell of the place was as much an assault on the senses as was sight of it. The waste of thousands of men, left to bake in the sun, combined with the odors of unwashed bodies, decaying flesh, and stagnant water, produced vapors that were nearly unbearable. "The stench from the prison could be perceived for two miles, and farmers living in the neighborhood began to fear for the health of their families," wrote one Georgia planter who lived in the area.[13]

One of the first dilemmas new inmates had to confront

Andersonville Prison did not contain any buildings, so prisoners had to make their own shelter. The wooden railing to the right was known as the deadline. If a prisoner crossed it, he risked getting shot by a guard.

was the complete lack of shelter from the sun, rain, and cold. The sun was hot and the rains frequent. "The month of June gave us twenty-seven days of rain—not consecutively, but so frequently that no one was dry in all that time," remembered Charles Hopkins, a prisoner from New Jersey.[14]

Although they offered little protection from driving rain, every able prisoner constructed some kind of crude shelter to protect himself from the sun. "The heat of the sun was so great that we used it to do the cooking," wrote Ezra Hoyt Ripple, a prisoner from Pennsylvania.[15] Ripple, like many others, built a makeshift tent called a shebang. Shebangs were constructed of bits of cloth of all kinds—blankets, old flour sacks, shirts, coats, even pants ripped apart. The pieces of cloth were then strung between sticks. One resourceful New Jersey prisoner and his friends made their shebang by sewing together "the sleeve and back linings of my blouse . . . our sugar and coffee bags, and . . . the flap of Hoffman's knapsack."[16]

Some prisoners, who did not have the luxury of extra clothing to use for a shebang, dug and crawled into holes in the ground. But these holes could prove deadly. Some caved in and suffocated the prisoners inside. And they were hardly a comfort when wet from rain. "Many . . . had been smothered in their 'burrows' made in the side hill in which they crawled to shield themselves from sun and storm, the soil being sandy, became rain-soaked, . . . chilling blood and marrow, life, flitted easily away, and left but little to return to clay."[17]

The shebangs and holes were horribly crowded together, with no streets or sense of order to them. By June the overcrowding had become so bad that an addition was built onto the prison. When the gate to the ten-acre addition was opened on July 1, there was a virtual stampede of prisoners trying to squeeze through the twelve-foot opening. Nearly thirteen thousand men passed through the narrow gate in just two hours.[18]

Even the most primary protection of all—that afforded by clothing—was a luxury to the Andersonville prisoners. They were wholly dependent on what they were wearing when captured, which often was not in the best of condition, and frequently was taken from them by their Confederate guards. Most had barely enough to cover themselves, and some none at all.[19] The Confederate guards, Kellogg said, did a good job of confiscating any pieces of a new prisoner's clothing that were worth anything. "I have seen them come in hatless, shoeless, without even their coats or blouses," he said.[20]

What little clothing the prisoners did manage to hang on to was soon filthy and in tatters. Ezra Hoyt Ripple offered one reason for their deplorable condition: The men often refrained from laundering their clothes to avoid weakening the fabric and thus shortening its life. "I did try washing my shirt once shortly after I came in the prison while the spirit of cleanliness was strong in me as yet," he said. "But I did not repeat it again while I was in prison. When I put that shirt in the wash it was an able-bodied shirt, it could even stand alone, but when it came out it was a poor, miserable, limp wreck."[21]

Another reason for the filthiness of the men was the condition of the water in the prison. A stream that flowed through the center of the prison was supposed to meet all of the men's needs for water. The problem was that at the head of the stream, the cookhouse dumped all of its greasy waste; then farther downstream, the open latrines (toilets called sinks) that were to serve the entire camp also emptied into it. The result was that the water was wholly unfit for either bathing or drinking. George W. Murray, a Connecticut soldier who was brought to Andersonville badly wounded, reported his surprise when he first asked a fellow prisoner for something to drink:

> He presented me with an old horn which answered as a drinking cup. But what was worse, the water that it contained was in no condition for either man or beast to drink. It had become stagnated, and a green slime had accumulated on it. This, then, was the water we had to drink, and the only water that was to be had within those limits.[22]

Albert Harry Shatzel, a cavalryman from Vermont, commented,

> Not half watter [sic] enough to drink & what we do get isn't fit for a Hog for it runs through the camp & every night & morning the cooks empty their greasy watter [sic] & filth in the Brook & the stench that arises from the watter [sic] is enough to suffocate aney [sic] comman [sic] man god help us.[23]

Some prisoners dug wells with sticks and other improvised tools, but they jealously guarded their precious liquid.

Because of the swampy, filthy condition of the stream and its banks and the dirty state of the men, vermin such as lice and maggots infested Andersonville. "Andersonville seems to be headquarters for all the little pests that ever originated—flies by the thousand millions," wrote prisoner John L. Ransom.

> Ground covered with maggots. Lice by the fourteen hundred thousand million infest Andersonville. A favorite game among the boys is to play at odd or even, by putting their hand inside some part of their clothing, pull out what they can conventionally get hold of and say 'odd or even?' and then count up to see who beats. . . . Some of the men claim to have pet lice which they have trained.[24]

While some prisoners tried to treat the vermin situation with good humor, it could also be gruesome in the extreme. As one prisoner wrote,

I tried to bear it but matters grew worse, till I hobbled out to

A crowd of prisoners waits to receive rations. Even if they were lucky enough to get food, the quality was usually terrible at Andersonville.

a guard's fire nearby and begged a firebrand. Taking the blazing pitch pine brand and going back into the tent, I took off my clothes and killed over 400 graybacks by actual count. They were as large as a very large kernel of wheat, and the scars where they bit me I shall carry to the grave.[25]

Ezra Hoyt Ripple wrote, "Horrible as it may seem to you, I have myself seen poor fellows lying out in the blazing sun, too weak to help themselves in the least, unable to turn themselves, lying face up, the maggots feasting on them and the lice devouring them."[26]

Even in the hospital, lice were a serious problem. Said Robert Kellogg,

> The [patients] scarcely ever wore any clothing at all, but a shirt, that they might keep as free as possible from the lice, which covered all their clothing. . . . Many men have died apparently from no other cause than that of being overrun with lice.[27]

Perhaps the most torturous aspect of life at Andersonville was the lack of food and the poor quality of the food that the prisoners did consume. All who kept diaries or later wrote about their experiences in the prison complained bitterly of the lack of decent food. In May, Ransom wrote,

> We get a quarter of a loaf of bread, weighing about six ounces, and four or five ounces of pork. . . . Rations *very* small and *very* poor. The meal that the bread is made out of is ground, seemingly, cob and all, and it scourges the men fearfully. Things getting continually worse.[28]

Sometimes there was slight variation in the food doled out—rice instead of cornmeal, beef instead of pork, an occasional serving of molasses or cowpeas—but the quality was usually inferior. Ohio cavalryman David Kennedy wrote of the rice he was issued one day, "Not half cooked, brought in in an old soap barrel, very strong of soap. [E]nough to make a body puke to look at it."[29] Ransom August Chadwick, a New York infantryman, wrote of his Fourth of July meal, "Drew fresh Beef or said to be fresh. But I called it rather Oald all Magotts and stunk enough to knock a man over this was our fourth supper a grate treate I should reckon after going without Reytions 2 days."[30]

Normally, the rations were issued once a day. However, as Chadwick made reference to, often prisoners would go a day or two without food. Rations were withheld for various reasons. For example, an entire company of ninety men would be denied their rations if one of their number could not be accounted for.[31]

The ration situation was made even more burdensome by the following facts: The men had no dishes in which to receive their scanty meals, and they were frequently required to cook their food themselves, but they were not issued enough wood to do so. Said Charles C. Fosdick of Iowa,

> We were put to our wit's end to know how to receive our rations. We had no vessels except our little coffee cans, and many did not have even these. Some would draw in their hats, mixing meal, peas and beef all together; others would tear out a shirt sleeve, tie a string around one end, and draw in it, and others would draw theirs in a corner of their blouse.[32]

John M. Burdick, a cavalryman from New York, wrote, "We don't have wood enough to cook half of what we get."[33]

Better food, usually obtained through trade with the guards, could be had—but at extremely high prices for the time. One prisoner recorded the following prices in his diary in mid-June: butter, two dollars for a small cup; salt, twenty-five cents for two desert spoonfuls; flour, one dollar to one dollar and fifty cents per pound; molasses, one dollar and fifty cents per pint; brown soap, three dollars per bar (equal to "about 1/3 of a Yankee bar").[34] Many prisoners, however, were forced to exist on the meager rations that were officially issued.

By the time he was rescued from Andersonville at the war's end, George Murray reported that he weighed only 73 pounds. When he enlisted, he had weighed 160 pounds.[35]

Robert Kellogg said that he had seen hundreds of men walking around the prison whom he estimated weighed no more than seventy-five pounds each.[36] One Northern officer, visiting the prisoners who had been liberated at the end of the war, recorded the following observation by a doctor who attended them: "The testimony of both men and officers was uniform as to the causes of their unnatural condition. These causes were, first, starvation, and second, exposure."[37]

Not surprisingly, sicknesses of all kinds were rampant in the camp. Dysentery, a painful affliction of the intestines, and diarrhea were the most common.[38] Many men also suffered from scurvy (a disease that rots the gums, weakens the blood, and produces large sores on the body) because of the complete lack of fresh fruit and vegetables in their diet. Those who had open wounds or sores of any kind usually ended up with massive infections and gangrene (decaying of body tissues). There was a prison hospital, but it was woefully undersupplied, with many of the inmates forced to lie on the bare ground and many more sick men denied admittance altogether. Hiram Buckingham, a prisoner who had been paroled for duty as a doctor's clerk in the Andersonville prison hospital, testified that

> a man never went in and came out alive, for usually he was so low upon his admission, that there was almost nothing to hope for, and in the second place, if a man had a friend or comrade to help him, he would not go in at all, for he preferred to die in the comparative quiet of his own tent, surrounded by such comforts as friendly sympathy could procure, rather than end his days where so much wretchedness was congregated.[39]

One Minnesota private later recalled the following about his time in Andersonville:

> The sight of all this misery, the starved, dying and half-naked humans all around, those with scurvy misshaped limbs, swollen limbs, swollen joints, and festering sores infected with gangrene, all contributed to make the newcomer so unnerved that he would soon get into a mental condition of despair out of which the ghost beacon of death seemed welcome.[40]

The deaths resulting from the sickness and starvation quickly reached massive numbers. By August and September, anywhere from eighty to more than one hundred deaths were reported each day.[41] Not only was death common at Andersonville, but the treatment of the dead was disrespectful and further deteriorated the men's morale. When a prisoner died, those around him immediately stripped him of his possessions and often of his clothes as well. The body was then carried out to the "dead house" outside the stockade, where stacks of corpses, their stench unimaginable as they baked in the sun, awaited burial. There was often competition among the prisoners for the "privilege" of taking dead men out to the dead house, as it

This scene was repeated quite often at Andersonville. A prisoner trying to retrieve one of his few possessions is shot after crossing the deadline.

gave them a chance to pick up a few sticks to use for cooking fuel. Prisoners let out on parole piled the bodies on open wagons, drove them to the cemetery, and there buried them in long six-foot-wide trenches, naked and without caskets.[42]

Many men, understandably, did not hold up well under such horrible conditions. Incidents of brawling, thievery, and even killing among the prisoners were commonplace. "Our own men are worse to each other than the rebels are to us," wrote one.[43] Quite a few prisoners went insane. "Some would beg for something to eat; others asked for wife, mother, children or other relatives," wrote Charles Hopkins.

> Some, in their delirium were home talking to their friends . . . and a goodly number were furiously wild, and had they been strong they would have been dangerous—not knowing their closest friend, trusting no one, raving and cursing in fearful language.[44]

Other prisoners tried to escape. One of the most common methods of escape was tunneling. Men would work for nights on end tunneling under the stockade with crude digging tools and carrying the dirt out in their clothes. By day they covered over the entrance. Robert Kellogg recounted several tunneling schemes. A few prisoners did manage to get free in this way, but most were turned over to the Confederate guards by fellow prisoners willing to turn traitor in exchange for an extra ration.[45]

Another escape scheme that was tried a number of times was posing as a dead man and then getting carried out to the dead house. A few of those willing to endure the horrors of lying in a pile of dead bodies for hours did manage to make good their escape in this way.[46]

The guards, helped by dogs, managed to catch most of those attempting an escape, however. There were over one thousand guards on duty at Andersonville. Most of these guards were members of the reserves, not regular troops, and as such were often very young (fourteen or fifteen) or very old (over sixty-five). On any given day, approximately three hundred guards would keep watch over the prisoners.[47] Some guards had compassion for the men in their custody, and gave them food for trinkets or money. Others—especially the young guards—were trigger-happy. They needed little excuse to shoot a Yankee (Northerner). They took full advantage of the rule that said any prisoner reaching over the deadline would be shot. One Georgia planter who served as an enlisted man in the first Georgia regiment wrote to his wife that some of the reserves had

> no more sense than to shoot them [prisoners] if they dare cross the line just to pick up a ball or empty a washpan. . . . Some of them would like nothing better than to shoot one of the scoundrels just for the fun of it. Indeed I heard one chap say that he just wanted one to put his foot over the line when he was on post, and he would never give him time to pull it back.[48]

In the eyes of most Andersonville prisoners, though, the worst of their Confederate keepers was Henry Wirz. General Lew Wallace, one of the members of the military commission who later tried Wirz, had not experienced his cruelty firsthand. Still, he painted a wholly unpleasant picture of the defendant.

> Wirz is a singular-looking creature. He has . . . prominent ears; small sharp-pointed nose; . . . eyes large, . . . very restless, and of a peculiar transparency, reminding one continually of a cat's when the animal is excited by scent of prey. In manner he is nervous and fully alarmed, avoids your gaze, and withers and shrivels under the knit brows of the crowd.[49]

Prisoners were much more harsh in their assessments of Wirz. Wrote Ezra Hoyt Ripple,

> His brows were contracted in an angry scowl and he stormed up and down the lines as he tried to get us in the position he wanted. One of our boys described Wirz as being the most even tempered man he ever saw, in that he was always in a rage. . . . He used very rough language to us and was very irritable and unreasonable.[50]

Another prisoner, John L. Ransom, said of Wirz, "Is a thoroughly bad man, without an atom of humanity about him. He will get killed, should we ever be released, as there are a great many here who would consider it a Christian duty to rid the earth of his presence."[51] Ransom had little idea when he made the preceding entry in his prison diary just how damaging his words would prove to be.

chapter four

HENRY WIRZ IS BROUGHT TO TRIAL

GEORGIA—As the Civil War drew to a close in the early months of 1865, tales of the treatment that Union soldiers were receiving in Andersonville had begun to circulate in the North. Some magazines even published gruesome photographs of former prisoners who were little more than walking skeletons. Many citizens were outraged. In fact, the desire of Northerners for revenge was so evident that many residents of south-western Georgia lived in terror of what the Union general William Sherman would do to them if his armies reached their homeland. One commented that it would be better for the Confederate army to take on the Yankees any place other "than here in South-West Georgia, for the horrors of the stockade have so enraged them that they will have no mercy on this country."[1] One woman from Wilkes County, Georgia, said she had heard that Sherman "did not intend to leave so much as a blade of grass in South-West Georgia."[2]

Stories of the horrors of Confederate prisons did a great deal to anger Northerners. Passions were aroused still further, however, by the tragic events of April 14, 1865. Just five days after Confederate general Robert E. Lee had surrendered to Union general Ulysses Grant at Appomattox Courthouse in Virginia, President Abraham Lincoln was shot and killed by a Confederate sympathizer. Although the assassin, actor John Wilkes Booth, was caught and shot twelve days later, the mood of the Northern states was, more than ever, one thirsting for revenge.

The last prisoners were leaving Andersonville late in April, but Captain Wirz stayed on at the prison with his wife and family. On the first or second of May, one of the conquering Union officers, Captain Henry E. Noyes, happened to stop in Andersonville on his way to another Georgia city. While waiting for his train to be refueled with wood and water, he saw a crowd of very sick Union prisoners being paroled by a Confederate officer whom Noyes took to be the prison commander of whom stories had begun to circulate. When Noyes reached the new Union headquarters in Macon, Georgia, he reported what he had seen to his superior, Major General J .H. Wilson.[3]

Wilson, meanwhile, had already begun investigations into Andersonville. Shortly after hearing Noyes's report that Wirz was still at Andersonville, Wilson received a letter from the prison commander. In the letter, Wirz begged Wilson to give him some sort of safe conduct (a promise that he could travel freely, without being arrested) or a guard so that he and his family might return to Europe. Wirz was afraid for his life:

> Men who were prisoners have seemed disposed to wreak their vengeance upon me for what they have suffered—I, who was only the medium, or, I may better say, the tool in the hands of my superiors. This is my condition. I am a man with a family. . . . My life is in danger, and I most respectfully ask of you help and relief. If you will be so generous as to give me some sort of a safe conduct, or, what I should greatly prefer, a guard to protect myself and family against violence, I should be thankful to you.[4]

Instead of granting Wirz's request, Wilson sent Captain Noyes back to Andersonville with orders for Wirz's arrest. Wirz and his lawyers later maintained that he had been unfairly arrested, as he had been promised "safe conduct going and returning to his home, and should not be arrested as a prisoner."[5] Captain Noyes told a different story. Noyes said that Wirz's wife and one of his daughters were crying and very upset at the arrival of the Union officers at their home. Noyes said that he tried to make it easier on the family by telling them that there was no need to worry. If, after questioning, it was clear that Wirz had done no more than his duty at Andersonville, that he had just been carrying out orders, he would probably be released and allowed to return home. However, Wirz was given no guarantee of safe conduct.[6]

Whatever he told Wirz's family, Noyes did, in fact, take Wirz into custody and then onto Macon for questioning. There, after about two weeks of questioning, Wilson had Noyes formally arrest Wirz and take him to Washington,

D.C., to stand trial. On the way to Washington, Noyes had to guard Wirz carefully, for whenever former Andersonville prisoners recognized him, they tried to get at their old over-seer to hurt him. Finally, Noyes had Wirz exchange his Confederate uniform for a black suit and had him shave his beard. Without such a disguise, Wirz would not have been able to safely complete the trip.[7] Upon his arrival in Washington on May 10, 1865, Wirz was imprisoned in the Old Capital Prison (on the site of the present-day Supreme

Henry Wirz was imprisoned at the Old Capital Prison during his trial.

Court building), where he waited while the government tried to decide what to do with him.

The government, fueled by a desire for revenge, had grand schemes in the works. Andrew Johnson, who had taken over as president after Lincoln's assassination, ordered the formation of a military tribunal to try Wirz. It was not Wirz alone, however, that the government wanted to try and convict. Government officials wanted even more to get at the highest-ranking officers of the Confederacy.[8]

When the charges against Wirz were finally published in August, they named seven high-ranking Confederate officers, including General Robert E. Lee and President Jefferson Davis, as co-conspirators with Wirz "to injure the health and destroy the lives of soldiers in the military service of the United States."[9] Wirz pleaded not guilty.

Although the court had been scheduled to begin proceedings the following day, the head of the special military court, General N. P. Chipman, received orders from the War Department to dissolve the court. Chipman was told to report to the office of the secretary of war, Edwin Stanton.

In Stanton's office, Chipman was instructed to prepare new charges against Wirz that omitted the names of former Confederate president Davis and members of his cabinet. Apparently, the War Department had gotten cold feet about naming the popular Jefferson Davis as a co-conspirator.

After lengthy consultation with other Army officials, it was decided that Chipman should reissue the charges against Wirz as they had originally appeared, only without the names of Davis and several others, and substituting the words *and others unknown.*

On August 23, 1865, the eight members of the court, all high-ranking United States Army officers, a judge advocate—Chipman—and an assistant judge advocate, were all sworn in. (In a military court, one man serves as both judge and attorney; advocate is another word for attorney or lawyer.) Then the new charges against Henry Wirz were read. There were two principal charges. The first was that he had "maliciously, willfully, and traitorously" conspired with John H. Winder, Richard B. Winder, Joseph White, W. S. Winder, R. R. Stevenson, "and others unknown" to "injure the health and destroy the lives of soldiers in the military service of the United States, then held and being prisoners of war . . . in violation of the laws and customs of war."[10]

This was the hotly debated conspiracy charge. The second charge concerned Wirz alone. This was a charge of "murder, in violation of the laws and customs of war."[11]

There were many specific details listed for each charge. Details for the first charge included such things as knowingly killing large numbers of prisoners by forcing their exposure to the heat of the sun, the dampness of rain, and the cold of winter; by forcing them to drink impure water; by feeding them "insufficient and unwholesome" food; by subjecting them to cruel and unusual punishments; by ordering the guards to shoot to kill anyone who crossed the deadline; and by using ferocious dogs to hunt down prisoners who escaped.[12]

There were thirteen specific details to the murder charge. These included charges that Wirz

- did with malice aforethought jump upon, stamp, kick, bruise, and otherwise injure with the heels of his boots a soldier (unknown name) belonging to the United States Army—the said soldier died. . . .

- With a certain pistol did feloniously and with malice aforethought, inflict upon a soldier (unknown name) a mortal wound from which the soldier died. . . .

- Did confine and bind with instruments of torture a soldier belonging to the Army of the United States (unknown name) and in consequence of such cruel treatment the said soldier died . . . .

- Did order a rebel soldier (unknown name) to fire upon a soldier, a prisoner of war (unknown name) inflicting a mortal wound from which the prisoner died. . . .

- Did incite, and urge ferocious bloodhounds to pursue, attack, wound, and tear in pieces soldiers belonging to the U.S. Army, and a prisoner (unknown name) was so mortally wounded that on the sixth day he died.[13]

Objections to the way in which the trial was being conducted began on the very first day. The attorneys of the well-known Washington law firm that Wirz had enlisted to defend him were so outraged that they withdrew from the case after the arraignment, or formal reading of the charges to the accused. The next lawyers whom Wirz hired, O. S. Baker and Louis Schade, also believed that the proceedings were highly unfair. Their response, however, was to make

Henry Wirz faced two principal charges. The first was that he had "maliciously, willfully, and traitorously" conspired with John H. Winder (pictured) and others "to injure the health and destroy the lives of soldiers in the military service of the United States."

several counterpleas on Wirz's behalf, including a number of very serious charges.

The first charge was that Wirz should have been protected from punishment by an agreement made between General Sherman and Confederate General Joseph Johnston, when Johnston surrendered to Sherman. The second charge was that Wirz had been promised safe conduct going from and returning to his home. The third charge was that a military court had no authority to try Wirz, as the war had ended. By trying him in a military court, the government was depriving him of his constitutional right to a jury trial. The fourth charge was that because Wirz had already been arraigned on almost exactly the same charges once before, he should be protected from being brought to trial again. Here, the constitutional protection against double jeopardy (being tried twice for the same crime) was cited.

Judge Advocate Chipman presented arguments to counter all of Wirz's special pleas. He said that the agreement between Sherman and Johnston was not intended to protect anyone from being prosecuted for crimes as serious as those with which Wirz was charged. He said that even if it was true that General Wilson had broken his own promise of safe conduct, that was an issue to be taken up separately and could not prevent Wirz from being tried for serious crimes. Chipman also said that a general had a right to take back his own order. To the charge that Wirz was being unconstitutionally tried a second time for the same crime, Chipman replied that he had not really been tried the first time; he had only been arraigned (charged).

Finally, regarding the legality of using a military court, Chipman responded at length and with passion. He traced the right of the president to form a military commission to the war powers given to him by the Constitution, which were his to use in time of war and "great public danger." Although the war was officially over, Chipman argued that it was still a time of great danger. As evidence that it was a very dangerous time and that use of the presidential war powers was justified, Chipman pointed out that the South was still under martial law (military rule), declared by President Lincoln shortly before he was killed.[14]

Although Chipman dismissed all of Wirz's pleas as invalid, the seriousness of those charges hung like a cloud over the proceedings, both during the trial and for years afterward. For decades, Wirz's sympathizers would maintain that his trial was a farce and an instance of gross injustice.

Yet, Chipman's word at the time was final. The trial would proceed. After Wirz pleaded not guilty to all of the charges and specifications, the judge advocate set forth the rules that would govern the preparation and presentation of the case.

chapter five

THE GOVERNMENT MAKES ITS CASE

TRIAL BEGINS—Clerks spent many hours writing letters to Andersonville survivors and staff from all parts of the country. Officers were sent on missions to states in both the North and the South to deliver subpoenas, or legal orders requiring that someone appear in court to testify as a witness. In this era before telephones, fax machines, and jet planes, preparation for the *Wirz* trial was a long and difficult procedure. Finally, however, it was time for both sides to present their cases.

The prosecution, the side in a trial that has accused another of wrong-doing, went first. Nearly one hundred thirty witnesses testified in all. They included not only former prisoners, but also Confederate officers and citizens. With respect to the first charge in particular, that of conspiracy, the testimony of former Confederate officers was quite important.

One of the most important documents of the trial was the report made by Colonel D. T. Chandler, who was assigned the duty of inspecting the prison and making a report on it to the Confederate government. Chandler visited the prison in July. His report showed that he was keenly aware of all of the major problems in the care of the Andersonville prisoners. He described the problems with the water supply, particularly the dumping of refuse into the stream by the cookhouse and its use as a toilet, the problems arising from lack of shelter; the lack of any systematic arrangement of the prisoners' tents; the insufficiency and poor quality of the food; and the problems arising from issuing rations uncooked without providing wood or utensils for cooking. Chandler especially deplored the conditions at the hospital and the lack of sanitation throughout the prison saying,

> The hospital accommodations are so limited that though the beds (so-called) have all or nearly all two occupants each, large numbers who would otherwise be received are necessarily sent back to the stockade. Many—twenty yesterday—are carted out daily, who have died from unknown causes and whom the medical officers have never seen. The dead are hauled out daily by the wagonload, and buried without coffins, their hands in many instances being first mutilated with an axe in the removal of any finger rings they may have.
>
> The sanitary condition of the prisoners is as wretched as can be. . . . No soap or clothing has ever been issued.[1]

Colonel Chandler concluded his report with numerous recommendations for improving the conditions at Andersonville. These included providing fresh vegetables, clothing, soap, medicines and bedding—and of course reducing the overcrowding by sending some of the prisoners away and not allowing any more to enter.[2]

In addition to his report being presented as evidence, Chandler himself testified as a witness for the prosecution. He said that he had urged General Winder, who was in command of all Confederate prisoner-of-war camps, to do something to alleviate the suffering of the prisoners at Andersonville. Winder's reply, which Chandler reported to the court, was shocking. According to Chandler,

> When I spoke of the great mortality [death rate] existing among the prisoners, and pointed out to him that the sickly season was coming on and that it must necessarily increase unless something was done for their relief,—the swamp, for instance, drained; proper food furnished them, and in better quantity; and other sanitary suggestions which I made to him—he replied to me that he thought it was better to let half of them die than to take care of the men.[3]

Chandler's reports, and others like it, were used to establish the fact that the treatment of Andersonville prisoners was the result of a conspiracy. High-ranking Confederate officials knew about conditions there and chose to do nothing about them.

A number of Confederate doctors made reports or issued statements that echoed many of Chandler's findings. One, a Georgia surgeon named Joseph Jones, had been given permission by high-ranking Confederate officials to spend several weeks at Andersonville studying the various diseases that afflicted the prisoners. Jones's description of the filth and stench at the prison was graphic and moving:

> The sinks over the lower portions of the stream were imperfect in their plan and structure, and the excrements were in large measure deposited so near the borders of the stream as

not to be washed away, or else accumulated upon the low boggy ground. . . . [it] accumulated in such quantities in the lower portion of the stream as to form a mass of liquid excrement. . . .

As the forces of the prisoners were reduced by confinement, want of exercise, improper diet, and by scurvy, diarrhea, and dysentery, they were unable to evacuate their bowels within the stream or along its banks, and the excrements were deposited at the very doors of their tents. . . . Masses of corn-bread, bones, old rags, and filth of every description were scattered around or accumulated in large piles.[4]

Dr. John C. Bates served in the Andersonville hospital from mid-September 1864 until the end of March 1865. In his testimony he spoke of the horrible condition of the prisoners in the hospital where he worked. "Although I am not an over-sensitive man," he said, "I must confess I was rather shocked at the appearance of things." He described patients without clothes and covered with lice, forced to live on food that was improper and insufficient for the sick. "It is my opinion that men starved to death in consequence of the paucity [small quantity] of the rations, especially in the fall of 1864, the quality not being very good and the quantity deficient."[5]

Bates was asked by a member of the court to state his professional opinion about "what proportion of deaths occurring there were the result of the circumstances and surroundings which you have narrated?" Bates replied, "I feel myself safe in saying that seventy-five per cent of those who died might have been saved, had those unfortunate men been properly cared for as to food, clothing, bedding, etc."[6]

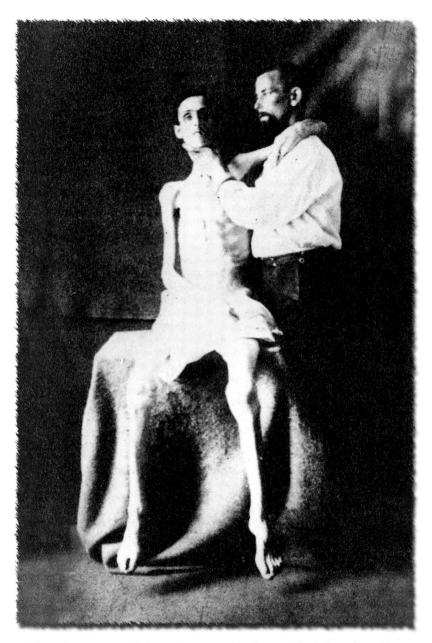

The mistreatment of the prisoners at Andersonville led to disturbing images such as this.

Still another Confederate doctor, Amos Thornberg, also testified that had the prisoners been properly cared for, many lives would have been saved. After describing the filthiness of the place, the lack of shelter, clothing, and blankets, and the poor rations, Thornberg concluded,

> Feeling we have done our whole duty, both in the eyes of God and man, we leave the matter to rest with those whose duty it was to furnish supplies and build up a hospital that might have reflected credit on the government and saved the lives of thousands of our race.[7]

The testimony of the Confederate doctors was supported by the testimony of about one hundred former Andersonville prisoners. The harrowing tales of life inside the prison were told from the perspective of those who suffered the horrible conditions directly. Some of their testimony was gruesome in the extreme. Boston Corbett was a soldier who, after being released from Andersonville, earned fame as the man who shot John Wilkes Booth, President Lincoln's assassin. Corbett testified:

> I have seen around the swamp the sick in great numbers, lying in a line pretty much as soldiers lie when they lie down to rest in line after a march. . . . I could see them exposed to the heat of the sun, with their feet swelled to an enormous size, and in many cases large gangrenous [infected] sores, without bandages to cover them, and the sores filled with maggots and flies, which they were unable to keep off. I have seen men lying there in a state of utter destitution, not able to help themselves, lying in their own filth. . . . That was the place where the worst cases generally were.[8]

While former prisoners testified about many of the same

matters discussed by the doctors, they also brought to life a side of Andersonville of which the doctors knew little. Many of the former prisoners spoke about the cruel and inhumane punishments that were used in the prison. During most of the testimony, Captain Wirz lay motionless on a sofa. His right arm had been giving him considerable trouble, and he sometimes felt so sick that court was postponed several days until he felt well enough at least to come and lie on the couch.

Numerous witnesses testified about the shooting of men at the deadline. Corbett described the portion of the deadline where the stream passed and the men went to get water. The rail marking the deadline was broken down at that point. Since the water nearest the stockade was the clearest,

> men would go in search of it as far as they dared . . . and, in some cases, they would get on the line without knowing it, because there was no actual line on the spot. . . . I have been within hearing of the sentinels who shot men on that line or passing it. I never heard them halt a man, or give him any intimation [warning].[9]

One prisoner who had been involved in burying the dead testified about how commonplace it was to come across a corpse who had died of a gunshot wound. He had had the job of burying the dead for approximately six weeks. During that time, he said,

> It would be pretty hard to tell the number of prisoners that I buried who had been shot, because it became so common a thing that we did not fix the number. I should say at least thirty, possibly forty, and it may be more. . . . The bodies would be brought in and the remark would be made, "Here

is another man shot." It became so common an occurrence that I did not take any notice.[10]

Robert Tate, a prisoner who had been a member of the Pennsylvania Volunteers, was one of a number of witnesses who testified that he had seen Wirz kick a sick man. He described an incident in which the prisoners had been ordered to fall into line for roll call at seven in the morning and were kept standing there, in the heat of the sun, until noon. One man was so sick that he fell down. His friends rolled him out of the sun and under a shed. "Captain Wirz came along and saw the man there and asked him what he was doing there," Tate testified. "The man told him he was sick and could not stand in line. Captain Wirz said, 'G[-]d d[-]m your soul, I will keep you into line.' He kicked the man and rolled him back to the line; the man lay there and was not able to stand up. In the course of two days the man died."[11]

Numerous former prisoners testified about the use of the chain gang. Jasper Culver of Wisconsin testified that he had seen, every day for over a month, twelve men chained together in a chain gang. Their legs were chained to thirty- and one hundred-pound iron balls, and they also had bands of iron riveted around their necks that were used to chain them to one another. "If one man moved," Culver said,

the whole twelve had to move. One of the file leaders was very poorly and seemed as though he could hardly carry himself without carrying ball and chain. . . . He caused a great deal of trouble by reason of his having diarrhea, and they all had to go with him whenever he was called.

Judge Advocate N. P. Chipman presided over the trial of Henry Wirz.

Culver said that he afterwards saw the sick man out of the chain gang. "I think he died three or four days after he was relieved from the chain-gang," he said.[12]

Many men spoke about other common Andersonville punishments, such as use of stocks, irons, and attack dogs. A former prisoner named Joseph Achuff told of being subjected to all three after attempting to escape. He was first rounded up by the prison hounds, which he tried to fight off bare-handed for almost fifteen minutes. "They caught me by the legs, and I carry the marks there today," he said. Once captured, Wirz ordered Achuff be put in the stocks. The wooden stocks held his head motionless and kept his arms uncomfortably outstretched. Achuff remained in the stocks, he said, for a day and a half.

> They pretended to have us in the shade, but I was kept in the broiling hot sun. For thirty-six hours I had nothing to eat, and but two drinks of water out of that dirty creek. When I appealed to Captain Wirz about it he told me to dry up, or he would blow my . . . brains out, that I deserved to be hung.[13]

After his release from the stocks, Achuff was subjected to yet another punishment. He was "ironed"—that is, he had iron shackles placed around each of his legs, and an iron bar between them, so that his legs were kept separated about eighteen inches apart.

In addition to the lengthy testimony about the brutal treatment that prisoners had received in Andersonville, there was also testimony to support the charge that Wirz had murdered prisoners, both by his orders and by his own hand. William Wallis Scott of West Virginia said he had seen Wirz hit a sick prisoner over the head and shoulders with the end of his gun hard enough that the man died soon afterward. The prisoner, seeing Wirz approaching, had asked the captain if he could be let out. According to Scott's testimony, Wirz turned around, gave the prisoner a sour look and said, " 'Yes, . . . I will let you out,' " and then struck the man with his revolver several times around the head and shoulders. Scott stated that three days later he had gone to see the man, to see how he was doing. "He was dead. He had died the night before." Scott was fairly certain that the man had died from the effects of the beating. "I saw him," he said. "He was pretty badly bruised around the head and face."[14]

George Conway of New York testified to having seen Wirz shoot a prisoner. The man had come down to the deadline to get some water. He had dropped his cup and reached under the deadline to retrieve it. "Captain Wirz shot him, the ball taking effect in his head," said Conway. "He died almost instantly."[15]

One lieutenant, Prescott Tracy, had witnessed an incident in which he saw Wirz order another soldier to shoot a prisoner. A new prisoner, who most likely did not yet know the rules of the camp, had put his head under the deadline. Wirz, who was nearby, had yelled up to the sentry, 'Why don't you shoot that Yankee . . .?' "At this point, the sentry fired, and the ball hit the man in the head and came out at the back of his neck. The man did not live," Tracy said. "He died right in the creek, and we pulled him out and buried him that same afternoon."[16]

Martin Hogan of Indiana testified that he had seen Wirz stomp on a man causing his death:

> I saw Captain Wirz . . . take a man by the coat collar because he could not walk faster. The man was so worn out with hunger and disease that if he had got the whole world I do not think he could move faster than he was moving.
>
> Captain Wirz wrenched him back and stamped upon him with his boot. The man was borne past me, bleeding from his mouth or nose, I cannot say which.[17]

Hogan testified that the man died shortly thereafter.

Some of the most moving testimony was delivered by a former prisoner who called himself Felix De La Baume. De La Baume claimed to be from France and a descendant of the Marquis de Lafayette (who had helped General Washington during the American Revolution). He spoke convincingly of seeing Wirz shoot a man who had fallen down in an epileptic fit. De La Baume spoke of seeing another die from being tied to a post with an iron collar around his neck and of hearing a young guard declare gleefully that he would now be granted leave after he had shot a prisoner at the deadline. De La Baume even offered as evidence drawings that he had made of various prison scenes. One of the drawings showed Wirz threatening to shoot a man. Another showed the dogs attacking him and his friend when they had tried to escape. One of the drawings was of a man wearing a ball and chain. Another showed a man bucked and gagged. (This is a type of punishment in which a person is tied up in an uncomfortable position.)[18]

The overall impression made by the witnesses for the

After prisoners died at Andersonville, they were buried in six-foot-wide trenches such as this. As more bodies were piled up in the ditch, the stench became unbearable.

prosecution was one that certainly seemed highly incriminating. Still, proper procedures were not always followed in the presentation of evidence. At one point, for example, a member of the court asked witness A. G. Blair of New York whether he had ever heard Wirz say that he would not give the prisoners rations even if he could. Blair responded, "I never heard him make that exact remark." He was asked the same question two more times. The second time, the witness again responded negatively. The third time it was asked, Wirz's lawyer objected to the questioning, claiming that Blair had already made clear that his answer was no.

Repeatedly asking the same questions, to get the same answer for effect, is valid grounds for objecting to a prosecutor's line of questioning. In most courts the judge would respond by telling the lawyer asking such questions to move on. However, Judge Advocate Chipman let the repetition of the question stand, and finally Blair did recall one instance in which Wirz had said he would not give the prisoners available rations.[19]

There were numerous other incidents in which objections to breaks with standard legal procedure were overruled by the judge advocate. It is impossible to say, however, just how much of the testimony against Wirz would have been disallowed if proper procedure had been strictly followed.

Wirz's lawyers objected to much of the testimony as well. They complained that the testimony regarding murder was too vague, since many of the witnesses were unable to furnish exact dates or names of the victims. Other former prisoners who testified were said to be unreliable because they had spoken under a sense of injuries done them, and they were encouraged by the enthusiastic response of those in the gallery. It was said that the Confederate witnesses either had been offered a reward for their testimony or had been threatened with punishment if they did not cooperate.

Although some of these charges could not be substantiated, critics of the *Wirz* trial did have some serious and legitimate complaints about the proceedings. One of those criticisms was the fact that some of the testimony was fabricated. At least one witness, Felix De La Baume, was found shortly after the trial to have lied on the witness stand. De La Baume made up the whole story about being French and a descendant of Lafayette. He was, in fact, Felix Oeser and was born in Saxony. He had lied about his name and his origins to cover up the fact that he had deserted from his regiment during the war. His testimony had so impressed the court that he had been given a written commendation signed by all of its members as well as a job in the Department of the Interior. When he was found out, Oeser admitted to having perjured himself (lied under oath), but then he disappeared.[20] Again, however, it is not clear just how much of what this witness had to say about events at Andersonville was also fabricated.

chapter six

HENRY WIRZ'S DEFENSE

TRIAL CONTINUES—In addition to protesting illegal and unfair procedures on the part of the prosecution, Henry Wirz's attorneys also presented a substantial case of their own. Compared with the prosecution's case, it may, however, have seemed modest. The defense had only thirty-two witnesses, compared with nearly one hundred thirty for the prosecution. Wirz's lawyers felt that the government did its best to prevent them from making the best and most complete presentation possible. O. S. Baker and Louis Schade protested the fact that they were not allowed to subpoena a number of witnesses that they wanted to use. Judge Advocate Chipman maintained that it was improper to permit men who may very well have been a part of the conspiracy to testify on Wirz's behalf. Chipman offered instead to allow as evidence signed affidavits (sworn statements) from all witnesses not allowed to appear. Baker and Schade refused, however, feeling it was important to have their witnesses appear in person. Since the judge advocate would not waver from his position, the defense was forced to do without the testimony of a number of men.

Many of the witnesses who testified for the defense offered reasons to explain why it was not possible for Wirz to have provided for the prisoners at Andersonville any better than he did. Lieutenant Colonel F. G. Ruffin served in the subsistence department of the Confederate Army. He testified about the scarcity of food throughout the whole Army:

> From the beginning there was more or less scarcity. . . . That scarcity commencing in that way increased in all sections to absolute privation. . . . The rations were reduced to a quarter pound of meat per day. The same reduction was ordered everywhere else. . . . The generals all remonstrated [complained], and said they could not keep their armies together on that.[1]

Dr. F. G. Castlen of the Second Georgia Reserves, who was stationed at Andersonville for six months, testified about the poor quality of rations that the Confederate soldiers at Andersonville received:

> The rations which we had for our own men were inferior, very inferior. Sometimes we got bacon, then again a coarse kind of beef, but in small quantities. . . . I heard a good deal of complaint that the rations were not sufficient. The men of my regiment, and particularly the sick, suffered a great deal from the want of rations, and the poor quality of the rations.[2]

The scarcity of food throughout the Confederacy was also an argument that figured prominently in the several books written after the trial in an effort to defend Wirz. In one of these books, entitled *Andersonville: An Object Lesson on Protection*, author Herman Braun offered figures on the production of wheat, corn, potatoes, and livestock, both in the North and in the South. He claimed that the figures "show the overwhelming superiority of resources in the Northern states compared with those states which, in 1864, practically constituted the Confederacy."[3]

Dr. E. A. Flewellen had an explanation for the use of unbolted cornmeal, that is, cornmeal made by grinding the entire ear of corn, cob and all:

> I called Dr. White's attention to the fact that the corn meal out of which I saw bread baked was not sifted; his reply was that he had made requisition but the sifters could not be had. . . . I know there was great complaint about the difficulty of getting sifters in hospitals and in the army too.[4]

This apparently was an excuse commonly used by the Confederate staff at Andersonville to explain to the prisoners the poor state of their rations. Witness Robert Kellogg remembered that the Confederate quartermaster had told him "that iron wire was so very scarce, that they could not procure enough to make the necessary sieves with which to clean their beans, before cooking, and therefore we must eat them as they were, dirt, pods, sticks and all."[5]

Flewellen, who was sent to Andersonville by the Confederate medical director of hospitals to inspect the prison hospital, also explained why the prison hospital was so poorly supplied. Flewellen said that he had found, during his inspection, a large supply of bed sacks and sheets in the office of Dr. White, the chief surgeon. When he asked

White why these had not been issued to the patients, he was told that, in the first place, White had not been able to get straw to fill the bed sacks, and that, even if he had, he would use neither bed sacks nor sheets because, until the hospital was finished, they would have to be put on the filthy ground. "He said that the sacks would soon be ruined; that they would be so filthy that they would never be fit to use when he should have succeeded in completing the hospital."[6]

Regarding the reason why the hospital had not yet been completed, Flewellen reported White as saying "that he was making efforts to fit [it] up—that he had not been able to get sufficient tools."[7]

Martin S. Harris of New York laid the entire blame for Andersonville at the feet of General Winder and the prisoners. A member of the court asked him, "You state that you have not anything to diminish with regard to the horrors of Andersonville as depicted by your comrades here?" Harris replied, "Nothing at all regarding the facts." The court member continued, "nothing excepting on the question of responsibility?"

"Yes, sir," Harris answered. When the president of the court asked him "On whom, in your opinion, is the responsibility?" Harris replied: "In my opinion General Winder was responsible, and also the prisoners themselves, by their conduct toward each other."[8]

In addition to offering explanations for the lack of supplies and facilities at Andersonville, another line of testimony that the defense attorneys pursued was to present evidence that Wirz had tried to improve conditions. A letter was presented, for example, in which Wirz complained to his superior about the poor quality of the rations he was obliged to give the prisoners:

> CAPTAIN: I most respectfully call the attention of the colonel commanding post, through you, to the following facts: The bread which is issued to prisoners is almost unfit for use, and increasing dysentery and other bowel complaints. I would wish that the commissary of the post be notified to have the meal bolted, or some other contrivance arranged to sift the meal before issuing.[9]

Baker and Schade also made a point of presenting witnesses who said that conditions were, in fact, not that bad at Andersonville. George Fechtner, for example, who served as an officer of the prisoners' own police force, testified at length about the abundance of goods available inside the prison. Fechtner painted an almost glowing picture of the bustling commercial life inside the Andersonville pen. "There were quite a number of storekeepers of different kinds there," he said. "I would be safe in saying there were a thousand of different kinds in the stockade." He went on to describe the wide variety of goods that could be had—for a price: breads, pies, cakes, ham and eggs, peaches, plums, grapes, overcoats, hats, shoes, and watches. "I cannot say that anybody suffered from hunger," he concluded. "The rations that I got when I first went there were sufficient for me to live on; after the first week I did not eat the rations at all. If anybody had money there he could get what he wanted to eat."[10]

Louis Schade acted as lead defense council for Henry Wirz during the trial. He believed that the proceedings were extremely unfair.

A number of witnesses for the defense spoke favorably about Wirz's character. They gave examples of acts of kindness he had performed. They also said that they had never seen or heard him mistreating prisoners. One witness noted that Wirz had paroled all of the drummer boys in the prison on account of their youth. "I know that about seventy, or probably eighty boys were paroled—brought out and put on nominal detail duty connected with the hospital," he said. "I know that they were permitted to go and pick blackberries, and Captain Wirz ordered them to be given tin pails to pick their blackberries in."[11]

Mary Rawson had visited the prison several times in the early months of 1865 to do what she could for an Iowa soldier she knew who was a prisoner there. Rawson testified that Wirz had always treated her kindly on her visits and that he had allowed her to bring food for her soldier friend.[12]

Former prisoner Augustus Moesner of Connecticut testified,

> I never heard of Captain Wirz shooting, kicking, or beating a Federal prisoner while I was at Andersonville. I swear positively to that; I saw him pushing prisoners into the ranks, but not that they could be hurt. . . . He would not push them in violently—a gentle push.[13]

The witness for the defense whose testimony perhaps carried the most weight was Father Peter Whelan. Whelan was a Roman Catholic priest who spent more than three months inside Andersonville prison ministering to those of his faith and to others in need of spiritual comfort. He was inside the stockade from 9:00 A.M. until 4:00 or 5:00 P.M.

every day from mid-June until the beginning of October 1864. Father Whelan certainly knew firsthand of the sufferings of the men there, and the honesty and uprightness of his character commanded the utmost respect. Yet when the defense attorney asked him, "From your intimacy with Captain Wirz while you were there can you state . . . what was his general conduct, as to kindness or harshness, towards the prisoners?" Whelan responded, "He was always calm and kind to me." The attorney then asked, "Was he to others, so far as you saw?" Whelan answered,

> Yes, sir; I have seen him commit no violence. He may sometimes have spoken harshly to some of the prisoners. . . . There have been some violences charged upon him here which I never heard of being committed by him. I never heard of his killing a man, or striking a man with a pistol, or kicking a man to death. During my time in the stockade I never heard of it. I never heard, either inside or outside, during my stay there, that he had taken the life of a man by violence. . . .

"If any such thing occurred must you not have heard of it?" asked the attorney. "It is highly probable I should have heard of it," Whelan replied.[14]

In addition to presenting testimony about Wirz's good character, the defense also used several tactics to show that the accused man could not have committed many of the crimes with which he was charged. One of these tactics was to argue that, because of his bad arm, he could not have carried out most of the beatings that he was said to have inflicted. However, there was disagreement among the testimony of various witnesses about whether they had seen him use his right or his left arm in instances cited.

Baker and Schade also tried to establish that Wirz was sick and absent from camp during the months of August and/or September, a time when several of the murders that Wirz was charged with were supposed to have taken place. Former prisoner August Gleich of Pennsylvania testified that he had been given the job of taking care of the Confederate officers' horses, including Wirz's mare. "Captain Wirz was sick once while I was at Andersonville," he said.

This is what the courtroom looked like during the trial of Henry Wirz. Wirz is lying on the couch (front, left).

I think it was in the month of August; Captain Wirz's horse stopped there in the stable while he was sick; nobody rode her then except Sergeant Smith; he sometimes rode her. Captain Wirz was sick about a month at that time; Lieutenant Davis was in command while Captain Wirz was sick.[15]

Other witnesses also testified that Wirz was sick in August and that Lieutenant Davis had been in charge of the prison that month. However, still others, including a Confederate doctor, said that they remembered Wirz having been sick in September or for part of August and part of September. Some also said that Wirz had not wholly given up his duties at the prison even though he was sick.

When the defense rested its case, things did not look good for Wirz. Louis Schade felt that all of his efforts to secure a fair trial for his client had been frustrated. He had not been allowed to put on the witness stand everyone he wanted. His objections to improper questioning of witnesses by the court had frequently been overruled. In addition, he was almost certain that some of the witnesses who spoke against his client had lied on the stand and gotten away with it. He felt completely demoralized.

The next step in the trial would be for both sides to address the court. According to custom, Schade, as attorney for the defendant, would go first. Normally, the defense attorney is expected to be ready to do his summing up shortly after all of the evidence has been presented. Schade, however, overwhelmed by the task he faced, asked the judge advocate for a two-week adjournment (postponement).

Chipman, feeling that two weeks was longer than could possibly be needed, told Schade he would give him twelve days.[16]

For Schade, this was the last straw. In protest over what he considered grossly unfair conduct of the trial, he declined to accept the counter-offer and walked off the job. Henry Wirz was left to face the most difficult part of his trial alone.

chapter seven

HENRY WIRZ'S LAST DAYS

VERDICT—At last, the long trial was almost over. It had lasted over two months and everyone was anxious for it to reach its conclusion.[1] The members of the court were weary. Press reporters, who had given the proceedings wide publicity, were impatient. Wirz himself found the suspense almost unbearable. There remained only the summing up by the two sides, then the deliberation of the court and the announcement of its verdict.

Normally in a military trial, if the defendant finds himself without an attorney, it is the job of the judge advocate to fill the position. N. P. Chipman, perhaps aware that he could not do justice to Wirz if he summed up for both the defense and the prosecution, instead ordered the three court stenographers to assist Wirz in the preparation of his final statement.

As sick and weak as he was, Wirz himself delivered his final address to the court. "I am no lawyer, gentlemen, and this statement is prepared without the aid of my counsel," he told the court.[2] However, Wirz went on to make a strong and well-argued statement that many lawyers would envy. The main plea he made was the same one he had been making since his letter the previous May to General Wilson—that he should not be held responsible for merely following the orders of his superiors. "A poor subaltern officer should not be called upon to bear upon his overburdened shoulders the faults and misdeeds of others," he said.[3]

Wirz also examined the various classes of evidence that had been presented against him in the case of the murder charge. He spoke indignantly about the quality of the testimony. "It cannot be expected, neither law nor justice requires," he said, "that I should be able to defend myself against the vague allegations, the murky, foggy, indefinite, and contradictory testimony."[4]

He singled out two of the specifications in particular for exposure of poor evidence. In the case of the alleged murder of a prisoner who went by the name Chickamauga, Wirz pointed out that the incident had been described by "at least twenty witnesses, and in as many different versions."[5] In the case of the murder of the soldier referred to as William Stewart, which George Gray had testified to, Wirz took advantage of the opportunity he had been denied during the trial—to call Gray a total fraud. "Wm. Stewart of the 9th Minnesota infantry is as much a creation of the fertile imagination of the witness who testified to his murder by me, as the conspiracy charged against me is a creation of the fancy of the judge advocate."[6]

Wirz closed with an emotional, eloquent plea:

> This court . . . is composed of brave, honorable, and enlightened officers, who have the ability, I am sure, to distinguish the real from the fictitious in this case, the honesty to rise above popular clamor and public misrepresentations. . . . I cannot believe that they will consent to . . . consign to a felon's doom a poor subaltern officer, who, in a different post, sought to do his duty and did it. . . . May God so direct and enlighten you in your deliberations that your reputation for impartiality and justice may be upheld, my character vindicated, and the few days of my natural life spared to my helpless family.[7]

Chipman followed with his closing remarks a day later. The judge advocate went on at great length. He addressed all of the complaints and protests that had been made by the defense. He spoke again of the legal justifications for trying Wirz in a military court. He also defended the conduct of the trial and dismissed any improper procedures he might have used as inconsequential: "It would be strange indeed if this record of five thousand pages, of sixty-three days of weary, laborious trial, presented no wrong rulings, no improper exclusion or admission of evidence in a greater or less degree pertinent to some issue made." Still, Chipman said, he could make the statement "with all confidence and with honest belief," that Wirz's interests had nonetheless been well served.[8]

He addressed the complaints about the vagueness of the testimony, saying that the prisoners had in many cases lost all track of what day, or even what month it was. They also witnessed so many horrible incidents on a daily basis that it should not be surprising if they were unable to fix with certainty the date of one in particular.[9]

Chipman explained the "laws of war," tracing the origin of the humane principles upon which civilized nations were supposed to conduct war back to the Bible and European philosophers. He declared that Wirz's argument that he was not to blame because he had just been following orders violated the laws of civilized warfare. "A superior officer cannot order a subordinate to do an illegal act, and if a subordinate obey such an order and disastrous consequences result, both the superior and the subordinate must answer for it," he said.[10]

The judge advocate also reviewed at length all of the evidence that had been presented, concerning the charge of conspiracy and the charge of murder. In this review he dismissed much of the testimony in Wirz's defense by pointing out that simply because the accused had done some kind things did not mean that he could not have been guilty of the crimes with which he was charged. "If in the course of one year's pursuit of . . . a stupendous crime indeed," Chipman said, "the perpetrator [person who did it] could show less than this prisoner has shown in his favor, he would not be entitled to the human name."[11]

Finally, Chipman made an impassioned plea to the court:

> Mortal man has never been called to answer before a legal tribunal to a catalogue of crime like this. One shudders at the fact, and almost doubts the age we live in. I would not harrow up your minds by dwelling further upon this woeful record. The obligation you have taken constitutes you the sole judges of both law and fact. I pray you administer the one, and decide the other.[12]

A large group of reporters covered the execution of Henry Wirz.

Decades later, the judge advocate would admit that he may have been harsher in his final address than was necessary. Writing in 1911, he begged pardon for "some extravagance of speech, some comments and criticisms which, in after years, may seem unnecessarily. . . harsh and severe."[13]

After the closing statements from both sides, Wirz was escorted back to the Old Capital Prison to wait while the members of the court deliberated. It did not take them long to reach their verdict.

The courtroom was packed with reporters and spectators as the members of the court and the judge advocate reassembled. Wirz, pale and haggard, had been escorted back from his cell by guards. The room for some time had been abuzz with excited whisperings. As General Lew Wallace, the court's president and spokesperson, rose to address Judge Advocate Chipman, however, all became deathly still.

"The court, being cleared for deliberation, and having maturely considered the evidence adduced [presented], find the accused, Henry Wirz, as follows," he began. Wallace went on to pronounce Wirz guilty of the first charge—conspiring "maliciously, traitorously, and in violation of the laws of war, to impair and injure the health and to destroy the lives. . . of large numbers of Federal prisoners." It is of interest that the court amended the original language of the charge to reinsert the name of Jefferson Davis as a co-conspirator.

The verdict in the case of the second charge, that of murder, was also guilty. Although in three of the specific instances that had been named, Wirz was declared not guilty, the court added three additional counts of murder—by means of vicious dogs—of which they also believed him to be guilty.

Wallace concluded with the words so many had been waiting to hear: "And the court do therefore sentence him, the said Henry Wirz, to be hanged by the neck till he be dead, at such time and place as the President of the United States may direct, two-thirds of the members of the court concurring herein."[14]

In military trials, all sentences that call for the death penalty go before the president for a final decision. In keeping with this policy, the verdict in the *Wirz* case was sent to President Andrew Johnson, along with a lengthy explanation of the facts of the case.

For Wirz, awaiting the president's final word, each day was one of mental and emotional agony. He never wavered in the belief that he was not guilty of the crimes charged. He worried terribly for his wife and daughters, however. Their family home had been destroyed during the war, and whatever fortune Wirz had been able to put away before the war was gone by its end.[15] Most of all, he wanted the dreadful ordeal to be over.

In hope of speeding up Johnson's response—and perhaps touching his heart and obtaining a pardon—Wirz wrote the President a letter that read, in part,

> For six weary months I have been a prisoner; for six months my name has been in the mouth of every one; by thousands I am considered a monster of cruelty, a wretch that ought not

to pollute the earth any longer. . . . But oh, sir, while I wring my hands in mute and hopeless despair, there speaks a small but unmistakable voice within me that says: "Console thyself, thou knowest thy innocence. . . ." Such has been the state of my mind for weeks and months, and no punishment that human ingenuity can inflict could increase my distress.

GIVE ME LIBERTY OR GIVE ME DEATH

The pangs of death are short, and therefore I humbly pray that you will pass your sentence without delay. Give me death or liberty. The one I do not fear; the other I crave. . . . Whatever you decide I shall accept. . . . Excuse my boldness in addressing you, but I could not help it. I cannot bear this suspense much longer. May God bless you, and be with you; your task is a great and fearful one. In life or death I shall pray for you, and for the prosperity of the country in which I have passed some of my happiest as well as darkest days.

Respectfully,
H. Wirz[16]

While Wirz's letter was on its way to Johnson, orders from the White House had already been sent to the War Department. The orders declared the president's approval of the findings and sentence and commanded that "the sentence be carried into execution . . . on Friday, the 10th day of November, 1865, between the hours of 6 o'clock A.M. and 12 o'clock noon."[17]

On the night of November 9, Wirz was visited in his cell by Louis Schade. Even though Schade had left his service, he remained the one person Wirz felt was sympathetic to his cause. Schade had come to bring him an eleventh-hour offer of a pardon from a member of Johnson's cabinet. The pardon was conditional, however. In exchange for being allowed to live, Wirz would have to agree to testify that the former Confederate president, Jefferson Davis, was guilty of the deaths at Andersonville. Wirz refused the offer.

"Mr. Schade," he said,

> you know that I have always told you that I do not know anything about Jefferson Davis. He had no connection with me as to what was done at Andersonville. If I knew anything about him, I would not become a traitor against him, or anybody else, even to save my life.[18]

Final adjustments are made to the rope before Henry Wirz is hanged. Before the execution could take place, President Andrew Johnson had to give his final approval.

Henry Wirz's last known communication was a letter written the following morning to Schade. In the letter he thanked Schade for all the attorney had done for him and begged him to do what he could for Wirz's wife and children. "I am confident you will not refuse to receive my dying request," he wrote. "Farewell, dear sir. May God bless you. Yours thankfully, H. Wirz."[19]

Not long after he wrote the note to Schade, guards led Wirz out of his cell and into the prison yard. There, he found himself amidst a sea of people—four companies of soldiers and some two hundred fifty spectators. The guards led him through the crowd and to the steps of the gallows that had been temporarily erected in the middle of the yard. As Wirz mounted the stairway to the platform, his ears were bombarded by the chanting of the crowd. "Remember Andersonville!" they yelled.[20]

While the noose was being placed around his neck and a hood over his head, Wirz addressed his final words to the hangman. He told him that he understood that the hangman was just following orders and said that he, too, had just been following orders.[21]

At 10:32 the trapdoor was sprung, and Wirz swung wildly from the noose until, unable to breathe, death over-took him.[22]

chapter eight

THE LEGACY OF ANDERSONVILLE

AFTER THE TRIAL—The conviction and execution of Henry Wirz was by no means the end of the debate about Andersonville and about who was responsible for the horrors that occurred there. In fact, in the years that followed the Civil War, it seemed that the *Wirz* trial aroused more controversy than it settled.

During the war many Southerners, especially those who lived in the state of Georgia, expressed sympathy for the prisoners at Andersonville and disapproval of the way they were being treated there. It soon became unfashionable, however, for people who lived in the former Confederate states to say anything critical of Wirz or of the prison administration at Andersonville. Reluctance to criticize the former Confederacy was eventually transformed into a shifting of blame for the Andersonville deaths onto the North.[1]

Former Confederate president Jefferson Davis did much to fuel this shift in Southern attitudes toward Wirz. In 1888 Davis wrote to Louis Schade, Wirz's attorney, asking him to do what he could to clear

Wirz's good name: "I have often felt with poignant regret that the Southern public have never done justice to the martyr, Major Wirz."[2] (Wirz had been promoted from captain to major just before the end of the war.)

In 1890, as one of the last acts of his life, Davis published an article in *Bedford's Magazine* about Andersonville. The basic message of the lengthy and influential piece was that the North was to blame, in several ways, for the tragedy of Andersonville. "It was not starvation, as has been alleged, but acclimation, unsuitable diet and despondency which were the potent agents of disease and death," Davis wrote. "These it was not in our power to remove. The remedy demanded alike of humanity and good faith was the honest execution of the cartel [exchange agreement]."[3] In other words, the chief cause of the suffering at Andersonville was the refusal by the North to continue exchanging prisoners.

Southerners claimed that General Ulysses Grant's refusal to continue the exchanges was based more on a fear of strengthening the Confederate Army than on a sense of injustice at Southern treatment of African-American regiments taken prisoner. They frequently quoted correspondence between Grant and General Benjamin Butler from August 1864 on the subject of prisoner exchanges. Grant wrote,

> It is hard on our men held in southern prisons not to exchange them, but it is humanity to those left in the ranks to fight our battles. Every man we hold, when released on parole or otherwise, becomes an active soldier against us at once, either directly or indirectly. . . . At this particular time

to release all Rebel prisoners North would insure Sherman's defeat and would compromise our safety here.[4]

Another argument that was made in Wirz's defense was that none of the other officers named with him as co-conspirators was ever prosecuted. Was Wirz tried and hung simply because he was easiest to get at?

In the 1890s several books were published with the aim of clearing Wirz's name. Those books included James Page's *The True Story of Andersonville Prison: A Defense of Major Henry Wirz* and Herman Braun's *Andersonville: An Object Lesson on Protection.*

The movement to clear Wirz's name, and at the same time restore honor to the Confederacy, gathered force as the next century dawned. In 1905 the Georgia division of an organization of southern women called the United Daughters of the Confederacy held its annual convention in Macon, Georgia. At that convention a resolution was passed to erect a memorial to Wirz in Andersonville "upon which a statement of facts shall be engraved in enduring brass or marble, showing that the Federal Government was solely responsible for the condition of affairs at Andersonville."[5] The resolution also proclaimed that Wirz had been "judicially murdered."[6]

The necessary funds were raised for the project, and in 1909, the tall shaft-shaped monument was formally unveiled in the center of Andersonville. The inscriptions on the monument declared Wirz's innocence and the federal government's guilt. They also condemned those who had

In 1909, this monument to Henry Wirz was unveiled in the center of the town of Andersonville. The inscription toward the bottom declares Wirz's innocence and the federal government's guilt.

participated in his trial, claiming that it had been illegal from the start and that witnesses had given false testimony.

Not surprisingly, the movement that resulted in the erection of the Wirz monument gained an angry response from many in the North. The head of the National Association of Union Prisoners of War appealed to N. P. Chipman, who was still alive, to make public the facts of the trial and stop what he saw as an effort to rewrite history:

> In justice to the memory of the brave and unhappy Union soldiers who perished miserably through the enforcement of that inhuman [Confederate] policy, we call upon you to place within the reach of the public the facts relating to this trial . . . . The necessity at the present time for an honest statement regarding the *Wirz* trial seems to be paramount, and we believe no one more fitted to perform this duty than yourself.[7]

Chipman willingly complied with the association's request. He wrote a long summary of the trial, most of which was composed of lengthy excerpts from testimony recorded at the trial. In order to accomplish the purpose for which it was written, Chipman published the book himself and had it distributed free of charge to libraries all across the country.

Northerners were not the only ones who found the movement behind the Wirz monument a source of embarrassment or anger. Father H. Clavereul, a Roman Catholic priest who had labored alongside Father Peter Whelan at Andersonville, wrote in 1910, "Not long ago a friend wrote me from Savannah that Wirz's admirers in Georgia intended to erect a monument in his honor. Now, I think, that the poor man is no more worthy of a monument now than he was at the time deserving of being hanged. His name should be forgotten."[8]

One Union Army veteran who heard of the movement to erect the monument questioned Confederate veterans that he knew to get their feelings about it. "A good many of them," he reported,

> had no hesitation in privately telling me that they agreed with me that the erection of the memorial to such a character could have no practical result except to smirch [stain] to a greater or less degree every memorial erected throughout the South to the real representatives of valor in the Confederate army.[9]

In the one hundred some years since the erection of the Wirz monument, the controversy over his guilt has died down considerably. While many today still find serious faults with the way his trial was conducted, few would go so far as to say that Wirz was wholly innocent, a man worthy of being called a martyr. This feeling is true in both the North and the South. In 1958 Georgia lawmakers voted against a resolution to repair the Wirz monument. Opposition to the resolution, interestingly, was led by a state representative named Ulysses S. Lancaster, whose great-uncle had served in the Confederate army at Andersonville. Lancaster told the Georgia Assembly that when Confederate veterans recalled Wirz and Andersonville, "it was with horror."[10]

In the North, noted legal scholar Alan Dershowitz agreed to write the introduction to a new edition of Chipman's 1911 book. In that book, Chipman admitted that he had written it "more in the spirit of the advocate than of the judge," that is, more as someone interested in condemning Wirz than in being impartial. However, Dershowitz noted that, even so, "the totality of evidence speaks for itself, and it speaks convincingly of Wirz's moral and legal guilt."[11]

Over the years, the interest in the controversy surrounding Wirz and his trial has gradually given way to a steadily growing concern with honoring the men who died at Andersonville. This concern actually began at the time of the Civil War itself. A prisoner from Connecticut, Dorence Atwater, had been assigned the job of keeping the hospital register of patients who had died. Atwater realized how much it would mean to the families of the prisoners who had died at Andersonville if, when the war ended, they could be notified of exactly when and where their loved ones had passed away.

Atwater secretly began to keep two copies of the list. When he left Andersonville, he took the duplicate copy with him. On it were the names of more than twelve thousand soldiers. After the war, Atwater teamed up with nurse Clara Barton, and together they managed to get the list published in *The New York Tribune*. They also secured the permission of Secretary of War Edwin Stanton to take a crew of workmen and artisans to Andersonville to identify the graves of the prisoners buried there and to make proper tombstones for them. At the time, they bore only small wooden markers with numbers on them. By comparing the numbers on the wooden markers with those on Atwater's list, all but four hundred of the dead were identified. The work crew then made wooden grave markers that bore the name, number, company, regiment, and date of death of each soldier. On November 25, 1865, three months after the crew's work was completed, Andersonville was declared a national cemetery.[12]

The cemetery began to attract increased attention around the turn of the century. A number of northern states, perhaps in response to the United Daughters of the Confederacy's efforts to have Henry Wirz declared a martyr, had monuments erected in Andersonville cemetery honoring their soldiers who had died there. Ten states altogether, including two from the former Confederacy (Tennessee in 1915

The Andersonville National Cemetery now occupies the area that was once home to Andersonville Prison.

and Georgia in 1976) have erected monuments in Andersonville.[13]

Over the years the cemetery has attracted thousands of visitors. The one hundredth anniversary of the Civil War and the publication in 1955 of the prize-winning novel *Andersonville* by McKinley Kantor increased the number of visitors still further.[14]

After the end of the Vietnam War, in which many American servicemen suffered as prisoners of war, a movement began to build a museum commemorating American prisoners of war throughout the country's history. Andersonville was selected as the site for the new museum. After almost ten years in the works, the National Prisoner of War Museum opened in 1998.[15] Andersonville now attracts more visitors than ever.

Henry Wirz and the legacy of his trial also live on, however. Wirz's trial was an important episode in the development of the laws of warfare. Above all, it helped to establish the principle that "simply following orders" can never be a valid excuse for committing war crimes. In the trials that followed both World War I and World War II, the *Wirz* case was cited whenever soldiers or officers tried to use the fact that they were simply following orders as a valid defense.[16]

Chapter Notes

Chapter 1. Drama in the Courtroom

1. 40th Congress, 2nd Session, House Executive Document, Vol. 8, No. 23, (1865) p. 398.

2. Ibid.

3. Ibid., p. 399.

4. William G. Burnett, *The Prison Camp at Andersonville* (Eastern National Park and Monument Association, National Park Civil War Series, 1995), p. 43.

5. *Facts and Figures vs. Myths and Misrepresentations: Henry Wirz and Andersonville Prison* (United Daughters of the Confederacy Bulletin of 1921), p. 30.

6. Ibid.

Chapter 2. American Prisoners of War

1. Lewis Paul Todd and Merle Curti, *Rise of the American Nation* (New York: Harcourt, Brace & World, 1968), vol. 1, p. 570.

2. National Prison of War Dedication Program (April 9, 1998), p. 35.

3. William G. Burnett, *The Prison Camp at Andersonville* (Eastern National Park and Monument Association, National Park Civil War Series, 1995), p. 11.

4. Ibid., p. 18.

5. Ibid., p. 38.

6. Philip Katcher, *Civil War Source Book* (New York: Facts On File, 1992), pp. 115, 120.

7. Ibid.

8. Burnett, p. 3.

9. Ibid, pp. 5, 22, 40.

10. N. P. Chipman, *The Tragedy of Andersonville: Trial of Captain Henry Wirz* (Sacramento, Calif.: N. P. Chipman, 1911), p. 407.

11. National Prisoner of War Dedication Program, p.34.

12. Ibid.

13. Ibid., p. 35.

14. Ibid.

Chapter 3. Conditions at Andersonville

1. Ovid L. Futch, *History of Andersonville Prison* (Indiantown, Fla.: University of Florida Press, 1968), p. 3.

2. Ibid., p. 5.

3. 40th Congress, 2nd Session, House Executive Document, Vol. 8, No. 23 (1865), p. 359.

4. Ibid., p. 357.

5. William G. Burnett, *The Prison Camp at Andersonville* (Eastern National Park and Monument Association, National Park Civil War Series, 1995), p. 4.

6. Futch, pp. 16–17.

7. *Facts and Figures vs. Myths and Misrepresentations: Henry Wirz and Andersonville Prison* (United Daughters of the Confederacy Bulletin of 1921), p. 3.

8. Ibid., p. 3; Futch, p. 17.

9. *Facts and Figures vs. Myths and Misrepresentations*, p. 4.

10. Ibid.; Burnett, p. 5.

11. Futch, p. 17.

12. Robert Kellogg, *Life and Death in Rebel Prisons* (Hartford, Conn.: L. Stebbins, 1865), p. 56.

13. A.C. Roach, *The Prisoner of War and How He Was Treated* (Indianapolis: Railroad City Publishing House, 1865), p. 225.

14. Charles Hopkins, *The Andersonville Diary and Memoirs of Charles Hopkins, 1st New Jersey Infantry*, ed. William Styple and John Fitzpatrick (Kearny, N.J.: Belle Grove Publishing, 1988), p. 77.

15. Ezra Hoyt Ripple, *Dancing Along the Deadline*, ed. Mark A. Snell (Novato, Calif.: Presidio, 1996), p. 40.

16. Ovid L. Futch, *History of Andersonville Prison* (Indiantown, Fla.: University of Florida Press, 1968), p. 31.

17. Hopkins, p. 96.

18. Kellogg, pp. 157–158.

19. Futch, pp. 31–32.

20. Kellogg, p. 189

21. Ripple, p. 23.

22. George W. Murray, *A History of George W. Murray and His Long Confinement at Andersonville, Georgia* (Hartford, Conn.: Lockwood & Co., 1867), p. 19.

23. Futch, p. 37.

24. John. L. Ransom, *John Ransom's Diary* (New York: Paul S. Eriksson, 1963), , pp. 91–92.

25. Burnett, pp. 38–39.

26. Ripple, p. 29.

27. Kellogg, p. 270.

28. Ransom, pp. 75, 81.

29. Futch, p. 35.

30. Ibid., p. 35.

31. 40th Congress, 2nd Session, House Executive Document, vol. 8, no. 23, (1865), p. 352.

32. Burnett, p. 4.

33. Futch, p. 36.

34. Jefferson J. Hammer, ed., *Frederic Augustus James's Civil War Diary* (Cranbury, N.J.: Fairleigh Dickinson University Press, 1973), p. 80.

35. Murray, p. 27.

36. Kellogg, p. 263.

37. Roach, p. 211.

38. Burnett, p. 12.

39. Kellogg, p. 249.

40. Burnett, p. 18.

41. Rick Marin, "The Infamous Stockade," *Newsweek*, March 4, 1996, p. 62.

42. Futch, p. 40.

43. Ibid., p. 41.

44. Hopkins, p. 95.

45. Kellogg, pp. 120–121.

46. Burnett, p. 12.

47. Ibid., pp. 3, 11.

48. Futch, p. 56.

49. Lew Wallace, *An Autobiography* (New York: Harper & Brothers, 1906), p. 854.

50. Ripple, pp. 16–17.

51. Ransom, p. 92.

Chapter 4. Henry Wirz Is Brought to Trial

1. Ovid L. Futch, *History of Andersonville Prison* (Indiantown, Fla.: University of Florida Press, 1968), p. 114.

2. Ibid.

3. 40th Congress, 2nd Session, House Executive Document, Vol. 8, No. 23 (1865), pp. 19–20.

4. Ibid., pp. 17–18.

5. Ibid., pp. 19–20.

6. Ibid.

7. Ibid., p. 20.

8. Futch, pp. 116–118.

9. N. P. Chipman, *The Tragedy of Andersonville: Trial of Captain Henry Wirz* (Sacramento, Calif.: N. P. Chipman, 1911), p. 32.

10. House Executive Document 23, pp. 3–8.

11. Ibid.

12. Ibid., pp. 3–5.

13. University of Missouri at Kansas City (UMKC) School of Law, Famous Trials Home Page © 1998, <http:www.law.umkc.edu/faculty/projects/ftrials/Wirz/Cont3.htm> (July 7, 1998).

14. Chipman, pp. 39–40.

Chapter 5. The Government Makes Its Case

1. N. P. Chipman, *The Tragedy of Andersonville: Trial of*

Captain Henry Wirz (Sacramento, Calif.: N. P. Chipman, 1911), pp. 66–67.

2. Ibid., pp. 67–68.

3. 40th Congress, 2nd Session, House Executive Document, Vol. 8, No. 23, (1865), p. 240.

4. Ibid., p. 622.

5. University of Missouri at Kansas City (UMKC) School of Law, Famous Trials Home Page, © 1998, <http://www.law.umkc.edu/faculty/projects/ftrials/wirz/xrpt2.htm> (March 15, 1999).

6. Ibid.

7. House Executive Document 23, p. 343

8. Ibid., p. 70.

9. Ibid., p. 73.

10. Ibid., p. 257.

11. Ibid., p. 388.

12. Ibid., p. 303.

13. Ibid., p. 163.

14. Ibid., pp. 194-195.

15. Ibid., p. 323.

16. Ibid., pp. 212-213.

17. Ibid., pp. 88-89.

18. Ibid., pp. 282-284.

19. Ibid., p. 344.

20. University of Missouri at Kansas City (UMKC) School of Law, Famous Trials Home Page, © 1998, <http://www.law.umkc.edu/faculty/projects/ftrials/Wirz/cont1.htm> (March 15, 1999).

Chapter 6. Henry Wirz's Defense

1. 40th Congress, 2nd Session, House Executive Document, vol. 8, no. 23 (1865), p. 646.

2. Ibid., p. 451.

3. Herman Braun, *Andersonville: An Object Lesson on Protection* (Milwaukee: C. D. Fahsel, 1892), p. 88.

4. House Executive Document 23, p. 471.

5. Robert Kellogg, *Life and Death in Rebel Prisons* (Hartford, Conn.: L. Stebbins, 1865), p. 226.

6. House Executive Document, p. 471.

7. Ibid.

8. Ibid., p. 596.

9. Ibid., p. 644.

10. Ibid., pp. 558–560.

11. Ibid., p. 696.

12. N. P. Chipman, *The Tragedy of Andersonville: Trial of Captain Henry Wirz* (Sacramento, Calif.: N. P. Chipman, 1911), p. 213.

13. House Executive Document, p. 537.

14. Peter J. Meaney, "The Prison Ministry of Father Peter Whelan, Georgia Priest and Confederate Chaplain," *Georgia Historical Quarterly*, vol. 71, no. 1, Spring 1987, pp. 15–20.

15. House Executive Document, pp. 428–429.

16. Chipman, p. 386.

Chapter 7. Henry Wirz's Last Days

1. Herman Braun, *Andersonville: An Object Lesson on Protection* (Milwaukee: C. D. Fahsel, 1892), p. 24.

2. 40th Congress, 2nd Session, House Executive Document vol. 8, no. 23 (1865), p. 705.

3. Ibid., pp. 706, 709.

4. Ibid., p. 710.

5. Ibid.

6. Ibid., p. 713.

7. Ibid., p. 721.

8. Ibid., p. 730

9. Ibid., pp. 802-803.

10. Ibid.

11. Ibid., p. 730

12. Ibid., p. 803.

13. N. P. Chipman, *The Tragedy of Andersonville: Trial of Captain Henry Wirz* (Sacramento, Calif.: N. P. Chipman, 1911), p. 427.

14. House Executive Document, pp. 805–808.

15. University of Missouri at Kansas City (UMKC) School of Law, Wirz Trial Home Page, © 1998, <http://www.law.umkc.edu/faculty/projects/ftrials/Wirz/Impact1.htm> (March 15, 1999).

16. Ibid.

17. House Executive Document, p. 808.

18. *Facts and Figures vs. Myths and Misrepresentations: Henry Wirz and Andersonville Prison* (United Daughters of the Confederacy Bulletin of 1921), p. 29.

19. Ibid., pp. 38–39.

20. University of Missouri at Kansas City (UMKC) School of Law, Famous Trials Home Page, © 1998, <http://www.law.umkc.edu/faculty/projects/ftrials/Wirz/executin.htm> (July 7, 1998).

21. Ibid.

22. Ibid.

Chapter 8. The Legacy of Andersonville

1. Ovid L. Futch, *History of Andersonville Prison* (Indiantown, Fla.: University of Florida Press, 1968), p. 118.

2. *Facts and Figures vs. Myths and Misrepresentations: Henry Wirz and Andersonville Prison* (United Daughters of the Confederacy Bulletin of 1921), p. 38.

3. Jefferson Davis, "Andersonville and Other War Prisons," *The Confederate Veteran*, vol. 15, no. 3, March–April 1907, p. 107.

4. Bruce Catton, *Grant Takes Command* (Boston: Little, Brown, 1968), p. 372.

5. *Facts and Figures vs. Myths and Misrepresentations*, p. 45.

6. Ibid.

7. N. P. Chipman, *The Tragedy of Andersonville: Trial of Captain Henry Wirz* (Sacramento, Calif.: N. P. Chipman, 1911), preface.

8. Ibid., p. 200.

9. Ibid., p. 13.

10. Futch, p. 121.

11. N. P. Chipman, *The Tragedy of Andersonville: Trial of Captain Henry Wirz* (Birmingham, Ala.: Gryphon Editions, Inc., 1990), reprint, preface.

12. G. Michael Strock, *Andersonville National Cemetery* (Eastern National Park and Monument Association, National Park Civil War Series, 1983), p. 6.

13. National Prisoner of War Dedication Program (April 9, 1998), p. 6.

14. Ibid., p. 7.

15. Ibid., pp. 7–9.

16. University of Missouri at Kansas City (UMKC) School of Law, Wirz Trial Home, © 1998, <http://www.law.umkc.edu/faculty/projects/ftrials/wirz/impact3.htm> (March 15, 1999).

Glossary

adjourn—To put off until a later time.

assassin—Someone who kills a politically important person.

cavalryman—A soldier who belongs to a unit that fights on horseback.

charge—An accusation.

Civil War—A war fought in the 1860s between the Northern and Southern states of the United States.

Confederacy—The name given to the union formed by the Southern states of the United States. These states left to form their own nation.

conspiracy—A secret plan to act together for an unlawful or harmful purpose.

conspirator—Someone who participates in a conspiracy.

dead house—The shelter at Andersonville used to store dead prisoners awaiting burial.

deadline—A railing erected eighteen feet inside the inner stockade of Andersonville; the prisoners were told they would be shot if they crossed this "deadline."

defendant—The person in a trial who has been accused of something.

defense—In a trial, the side being accused of a crime.

dysentery—A painful affliction of the intestines, with symptoms similar to those of diarrhea.

enlisted man—A soldier who volunteers to serve in an army.

gangrene—A condition in which tissue in a part of the body decays.

indict—To formally accuse someone of a crime.

infantryman—A foot soldier.

irons—A device used for punishment, consisting of heavy iron rings put around the neck, wrists, and/or ankles.

judge advocate—A person in a military court who serves as both judge and as attorney for one of the two sides.

martial law—Military rule.

minister—A person sent to a foreign country to represent his or her government.

mortality—Death.

parole—A prisoner of war's promise to take no further part in the fighting in exchange for his freedom.

perjure—To lie under oath.

prosecution—The person or organization (usually the government) that begins and carries out legal proceedings against another person in a trial.

prosecutor—The individual responsible for carrying out the prosecution of an accused person in court.

ration—A fixed daily allowance of something received by soldiers, most commonly an allowance of food.

Rebel—A member of the Confederacy, especially of the Confederate army.

safe conduct—A promise that one will be able to travel to a particular destination without being taken into custody.

scurvy—A disease that results from too little vitamin c, and that causes weakness, spongy gums, bleeding, and other symptoms.

shebang—A makeshift tent built of sticks and whatever bits of cloth or board can be found.

sink—In Civil War times, an outdoor toilet.

stocks—Devices that held a person's head and arms and/or feet so that they could not be moved; it was used for punishment.

subpoena—A legal order requiring that someone appear in court to testify as a witness.

testify—To make a statement under oath in court.

testimony—A statement made under oath by a witness in court.

treason—A betrayal of one's country.

Union—The term used to refer to the Northern states during the Civil War; it is also used to describe all of the states of the United States together.

witness—Someone who makes a statement under oath in court.

Yankee—A term used to refer to someone from one of the Northern states of the United States.

Further Reading

Gay, Kathlyn and Martin K. Gay. *Civil War*. Brookfield, Conn.: Twenty-First Century Books, Inc., 1995.

Haughen, David and Lori Shein, eds. *The Civil War*. San Diego: Greenhaven Press, Inc., 1998.

Kent, Zachary. *The Civil War: "A House Divided."* Hillside, N.J.: Enslow Publishers, Inc., 1994.

Sandler, Martin W. *Civil War*. New York: HarperCollins Children's Books, 1996.

Ziff, Marsha. *Reconstruction Following the Civil War in American History*. Berkeley Heights, N.J.: Enslow Publishers, Inc., 1999.

Internet Addresses

Andersonville National Historic Site
<http://www.nps.gov/ande/>

Andersonville Civil War Prison—Historical Background
<http://www.cr.nps.gov/seac/histback.htm>

The *Wirz* Trial Home Page—University of Missouri at Kansas City (UMKC) School of Law
<http://www.law.umkc.edu/faculty/projects/ftrials/wirz/wirz.htm>

Index